WARTS

ELAINE LANDAU

Marshall Cavendish
Benchmark
New York

Expert Reader: Dr. Stuart E. Beeber of Chappaqua Pediatrics, Chappaqua, New York

Published by Marshall Cavendish Benchmark
An imprint of Marshall Cavendish Corporation

Website: www.marshallcavendish.us

This publication represents the opinions and views of the author based on Elaine Landau's personal experience, knowledge, and research. The information in this book serves as a general guide only. The author and publisher have used their best efforts in preparing this book and disclaim liability rising directly and indirectly from the use and application of this book.

Other Marshall Cavendish Offices:
Marshall Cavendish International (Asia) Private Limited, 1 New Industrial Road, Singapore 536196 • Marshall Cavendish International (Thailand) Co Ltd. 253 Asoke, 12th Flr, Sukhumvit 21 Road, Klongtoey Nua, Wattana, Bangkok 10110, Thailand • Marshall Cavendish (Malaysia) Sdn Bhd, Times Subang, Lot 46, Subang Hi-Tech Industrial Park, Batu Tiga, 40000 Shah Alam, Selangor Darul Ehsan, Malaysia

Marshall Cavendish is a trademark of Times Publishing Limited
All websites were available and accurate when this book was sent to press.

Library of Congress Cataloging-in-Publication Data
Landau, Elaine.
Warts / by Elaine Landau.
p. cm. — (Head-to-toe health)
Includes index.
Summary: "Provides basic information about warts and their prevention"—Provided by publisher.
    ISBN 978-0-7614-4836-5
    1. Warts—Juvenile literature. I. Title.
    RL471.L36 2010
    616.5'44—dc22
    2009030916

Editor: Joy Bean
Publisher: Michelle Bisson
Art Director: Anahid Hamparian
Series Designer: Alex Ferrari

Photo research by Candlepants Incorporated

Cover Photo: Erich Schrempp / Photo Researchers Inc.

The photographs in this book are used by permission and through the courtesy of:*Getty Images*: David Young-Wolff, 4; Steve Satushek, 7; 3DClinic, 9; CMSP, 10; Darren Robb, 13; Peter Cade, 15, 21. *Photo Researchers Inc.*: Biophoto Associates, 12; Mark Clarke, 17; PHANIE, 19. *Alamy Images*: Radius Images, 23; Medical-on-Line, 25.

Printed in Malaysia (T)

1 3 5 6 4 2

CONTENTS

WARTS AND WITCHES

Picture an old, ugly witch. Imagine that she just stepped out of a really scary fairy tale. The witch wears a pointy black hat and flies around on a broomstick. She has beady eyes and a number of missing teeth.

Of course, no truly terrible witch would be complete without a few large warts. There might be one wart on her nose and a couple more on her chin.

This witch is the kind of creature we usually think of as having warts. You never picture warts on a beauty queen or the nation's First Lady. Yet believe it or not, anyone can have warts. They have nothing to do with being ugly, pretty, or important. They have nothing to do with being good or evil either.

THE TRUTH ABOUT WARTS

In real life, all sorts of people get warts. People in different parts of the world get them. People of all races, sizes, and

◀ Remember the witches in scary fairy tales? They usually have large warts.

ages get them. Children tend to get more warts than adults do. At one time or another, nearly half of all children will have warts. Some children get lots of warts. Others grow up without ever having a single one.

This is a book about warts. It's not a fairy tale, so don't expect to find warty witches on these pages. Everything you read here is true. Do you want the real deal on warts? If so, just keep reading.

DON'T TOUCH THAT TOAD!

Can you get warts from touching a toad?
Some toads do have skin covered with lumps
and bumps. But the answer is no. You can even
hold a toad and not get warts.

ALL ABOUT WARTS

If you get warts, this might be your first question: What are these strange things on my body? You weren't born with a bunch of bumps that look like tiny, badly shaped cauliflowers!

Warts may look scary—especially if they make you think of witches or toads. But there's really nothing to be afraid of. A wart is just a harmless skin growth. Warts don't suddenly pop up magically on your skin, either. They are caused by a **virus**.

CAUSED BY A WHAT?

Viruses are germs. They are among the smallest germs on Earth. Viruses are so small that you need a special microscope to see them. More than 300 billion viruses could fit on the point of your pencil. That's really tiny.

Viruses are small, but they can still cause problems. Some viruses cause AIDS, measles, chicken pox, and the flu. Luckily, warts are not as serious as any of these sicknesses. Having warts won't make you sick. In most cases, warts don't hurt, either.

How much do you already know about the viruses that cause warts? Read the following statement, and decide if it is true or false:

Warts are pretty much alike. Only one virus causes them all.

Did you answer False? Then you're on the right track. About sixty kinds of viruses cause warts. All of these viruses are members of the **human papillomavirus (HPV)** group.

Warts come in lots of different shapes and sizes. Different **strains** of HPV cause different kinds of warts. You can also find warts on different parts of the body. Let's take a closer look at the most common warts. You might already know some of these.

COMMON WARTS

Common warts most often show up on

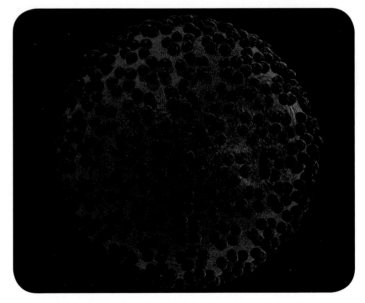

This is how the HPV virus looks under a microscope.

your hands and fingers. Lots of times they appear around your fingernails, but you might also see them on the back of your hand. Common warts are shaped like domes, and they feel rough. These warts tend to be a grayish brown color.

Have you ever seen common warts with little black dots? The dots look like seeds. That's why these warts are sometimes called seed warts. But the dots aren't seeds at all. These spots are really **blood vessels** that have grown into the wart to supply it with blood.

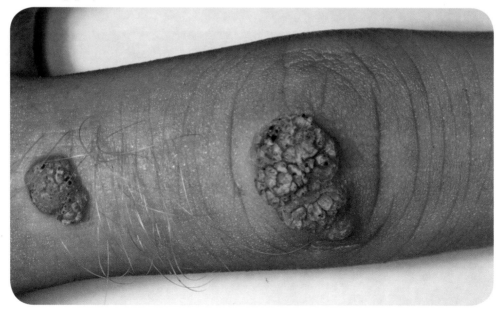

A close-up view of two common warts. See the tiny black dots? Those are the blood vessels that supply the warts with blood.

FLAT WARTS

Kids get flat warts more often than grown-ups do. That may be why flat warts are also known as **juvenile**, or kids', warts. Flat warts aren't very big. They are small and usually show up in bunches. You might have twenty-five or a hundred of these tiny warts at one time.

Flat warts are flatter and smoother than common warts. Some flat warts are light brown, while others are pink or even yellow. Kids most often get flat warts on their faces. Yet sometimes these warts also show up on knees, hands, and other body parts.

DO WARTS HAVE ROOTS?

You might have heard that warts have roots. This just isn't true. The viruses that cause warts only **infect** the top layer of your skin. This top layer of skin grows rapidly and forms a wart. The bottom of a wart is smooth and rootless.

FOOT WARTS

Did you know that you can get warts on the bottoms of your feet? These warts are known as **plantar warts**, or foot warts. Planter warts are flat. There's a reason for that. When you stand or walk, you step on these warts. That pushes them back into the skin and flattens them. Like common warts, plantar warts have small black spots on them.

Unlike most warts, plantar warts can really hurt. That's because you are squashing them as you stand and walk. Some people say it's like having a pebble in your shoe.

FILIFORM WARTS

When you hear the word *wart*, you probably think of a filiform wart. This is the kind of wart that scary storybook witches have. A filiform wart is flesh-colored, long, and slender. Fingerlike pieces stick out of these warts. Filiform warts usually grow on the nose, chin, and eyelids, as well as around the eyes and lips. People of any age can get these warts, but they are most common among older children.

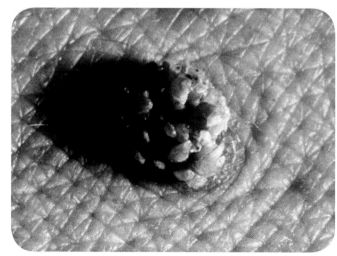

Filiform warts are recognizable because of the pieces that stick out from them.

DREAD THE SPREAD

Oh, no! You never thought it would happen, but it did. You've got a bunch of warts near your fingernails. They turned up one day and slowly grew bigger. You've never had warts before, and you don't want them now. How did this happen to you? You need some answers.

HERE COME THE ANSWERS

You can get a virus that causes warts in many different ways. One way is through direct contact with someone who has warts. If you touch a wart on your friend's hand, the virus can infect you, too.

The viruses that cause warts enter through your skin. Do you bite your nails or pick at your **cuticles**?

Biting your fingernails and cuticles can cause skin to break. A virus can easily enter broken skin.

You are more likely to be infected if your skin has been cut or broken in some way. The virus easily enters skin that is moist, peeling, or cracked.

Warts don't show up right away. They have a long **incubation period**. That's the amount of time between when you get infected and when you actually see the wart. It can take from one to eight months before the wart appears. That makes it hard to know how you got infected to begin with.

You might also have indirect contact with viruses that cause warts. Let's say one of your classmates has warts on his hands, and he uses the handrail when he walks downstairs. Now the virus is on the handrail. Seconds later, you walk down the steps and hold the same rail. Months later, warts pop up on your hand. The same thing can happen when someone with warts uses a doorknob, telephone, or toy.

YOU INFECTED WHO?

If you already have warts, is it possible to spread them to other places on your body? The answer is yes. That's why it's important not to scratch or pick at a wart and then touch another part of your body.

YOUR IMMUNE SYSTEM AND WARTS

Germs are all around us. So why do some people get warts and not others? It may have to do with their **immune systems**. Everyone's body has an immune system. Your immune system is your body's defense system. It attacks viruses that get inside your body.

Some people have stronger immune systems than others. At times, your immune system might get weak. For example, some treatments for cancer weaken the immune system. A very poor diet can do this, too. Diseases like AIDS also attack the immune system. People with weak immune systems are more likely to get warts.

People with weak immune systems are more likely to become ill as well as get warts.

Getting Rid of Warts

Nobody wants warts on their body. If you get them, you'll want them to go away. Yet you might know people who have had warts for years. So can you ever really get rid of them? The answer is yes.

OFF TO THE DOCTOR

If you think you have warts, it's a good idea to see your doctor. It's important to make sure that you have warts and not another type of skin growth. Your doctor will probably be able to see if you have warts by how they look and where they are on your body. In some cases, the doctor may want to **biopsy**, or take a sample of, the wart. Then the doctor can test the wart to make sure it's not something else.

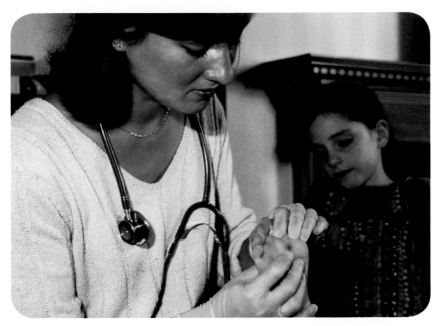

Here a doctor examines a young girl's foot for warts.

There are different ways to deal with warts. Your doctor might tell you to do nothing at all—in most cases, warts go away on their own. Your immune system wins out, and you're wart-free! Some warts disappear in a week or two without treatment. Others can take two years or more to go away.

I CAN'T STAND THOSE WARTS

What if you don't want to wait for your warts to go away? You really dislike the way they look and feel on your skin. Is there hope for you? You bet there is. Here are some of the things that you can do.

MEDICINES

People use different types of medicine to get rid of warts. You can buy some of them over the counter at drugstores. Others must be **prescribed**, or ordered by a doctor. Wart medicines can be liquid drops, gels, pads, or plasters. You should not use them by yourself. A responsible adult should apply the medicine to your warts.

Do you have lots of patience? You'll need it if you're dealing with warts. Often you have to use wart-removal medicine over weeks or even months. There are no guarantees, either. Sometimes the treatments work, and sometimes they don't.

TAPE ON A WART

Do you want to hear about a really strange way to remove warts? Just cover them with duct tape for a few weeks. Researchers have found that in some cases this really works. It seems that the tape cuts off the wart's air supply.

FREEZING OFF THE WART

A doctor must do this type of wart removal. Don't let the word *freezing* upset you. The doctor doesn't stick your whole body in a freezer.

Instead, the doctor performs **cryotherapy**. First, the doctor places a chemical on the wart to freeze it. Some people say it feels like an ice cube is stuck to your skin, but the feeling doesn't last long. The chemical freezes and kills the wart. You might need a few freezing treatments before the wart is completely gone.

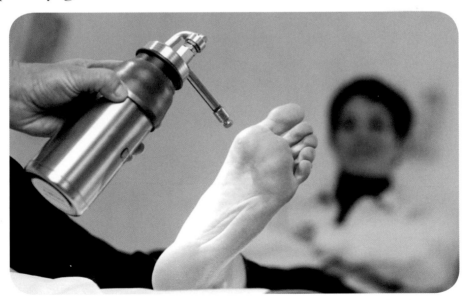

In this picture, a doctor freezes off the wart on a patient's foot.

LASER TREATMENTS

When other wart-removal treatments fail, your doctor might try **laser** treatments. With this method, the doctor applies a small laser beam to the wart. The laser beam kills the blood vessels that feed the wart. Some warts need only one treatment. Others need a few.

COMING AROUND AGAIN

Sometimes warts seem to return almost as soon as they're gone. This is often due to the old warts that have been removed. Before they were removed, these warts shed the virus onto other areas of your skin. To stop this cycle from repeating, treat the new warts as soon as you spot them. Then they will have little time to shed the virus, too.

No Warts for Me, Please

It's summertime, and you're at the beach with your friend. The sun is sizzling, and the sand is hot. You brought your flip-flops, but your friend didn't.

Now your friend is thirsty and wants to go to the refreshment stand for a soda. But he doesn't want to walk barefoot on the hot sand. He asks if he can borrow your flip-flops. Should you let him?

Hopefully, you say no. Lending your shoes to

Want to avoid warts? Don't share your shoes with others.

someone is a really bad idea. If your friend has warts on his feet, the virus can get on your flip-flops. When you put them on afterward, you might get the virus.

Here are some things you can do to stay wart-free. All these tips are easy to follow. Often it's just a matter of being aware and being a little extra careful.

SOME THINGS ARE NOT FOR SHARING

Share good times and laughter with your friends. But pass on sharing shoes, socks, and towels. If you share these things with someone who has warts, you could be in trouble. You've greatly increased your chances of getting warts, too. Not sharing personal items does not make you a bad friend. You're simply someone with healthy habits.

BEWARE OF GOING BAREFOOT

It can get hot in the summer. You may be tempted to kick off your shoes and go barefoot. This isn't a good idea in public places. Lots of kids get warts on their feet when they go barefoot around swimming pools. Teens often come in contact with HPV on locker room floors.

What's wrong with this picture? The boy should not be barefoot. Always wear shoes around swimming pools and locker rooms to avoid warts.

KEEP YOUR FEET SWEET

The viruses that cause warts thrive in warm, moist places. So it's a good idea to keep your feet dry. Dry them well after a bath or shower.

Do your feet get very sweaty? If so, wear socks that take in much of the moisture. Try not to irritate the soles of your feet, either. Warts grow more easily if your skin has been damaged in some way.

PICKING OR BITING IS A NO-NO!

Try not to bite or pick at your fingernails. These habits make you more likely to get warts on your hands. If you already have warts, don't scratch or pick at them. You can end up spreading the virus to other parts of your body. If you do touch or rub your warts, wash your hands with soap afterward.

STAY HEALTHY AND BE STRONG

Stay healthy, and keep your immune system strong. That means eating a proper diet and getting enough sleep. Try to exercise daily, and drink plenty of fluids. Keep your body in tip-top shape. You're likely to have fewer colds—and fewer warts, too!

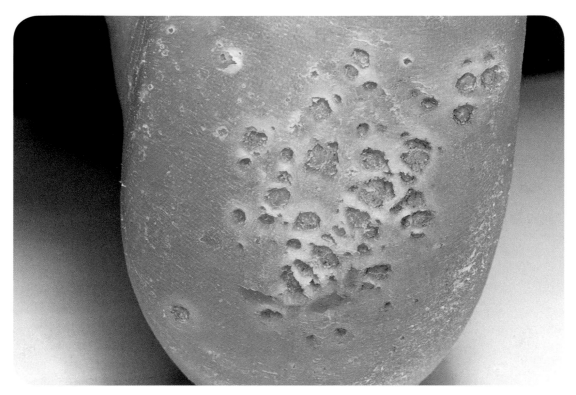

Here's a close-up look at plantar warts. Don't scratch these warts, even if they itch. You don't want to spread them to another part of your body.

These easy-to-do steps can go a long way toward helping you avoid warts. That doesn't mean you'll never get a wart. But you'll be doing everything you can to stay wart-free. That's a big step in the right direction.

GLOSSARY

biopsy — to remove a piece of tissue in order to study it

blood vessels — narrow tubes through which blood flows

cryotherapy — a medical procedure in which a doctor uses a chemical to freeze a part of the body

cuticles — layers of dead skin at the edges of fingernails and toenails

human papillomavirus (HPV) — strains of viruses that cause warts

immune systems — systems that protects the body against disease

incubation period — the time between when germs attack your body and when the signs of disease appear

infect — to enter the body and cause a disease or other sickness

juvenile — having to do with young people

laser — a device that makes a beam of light

plantar warts — flat warts that usually appear on the bottoms of feet

prescribed — ordered for a patient by a doctor

strains — particular types of viruses

virus — a germ that is too small to be seen without a special microscope

FIND OUT MORE

BOOKS

Johnson, Rebecca L. *Daring Cell Defenders*. Minneapolis, MN: Millbrook Press, 2008.

Parker, Steve. *Microlife That Makes Us Ill*. Chicago: Raintree, 2006.

Rosenberg, Pam. *Blecch! Icky, Sticky, Gross Stuff in Your School*. Mankato, MN: Child's World, 2008.

Thames, Susan. *Our Immune System*. Vero Beach, FL: Rourke Publishing, 2008.

DVDS

All About Health & Hygiene. Schlessinger Media, 2006.

Body Mechanics: Superheroes of the Human Body. Library Video Company, 2006.

WEBSITES

Be a Germ Stopper

www.cdc.gov/germstopper

Check out this website to learn more about how you can keep
yourself healthy.

What's Up With Warts?

www.kidshealth.org/kid/ill_injure/aches/warts.html

Check out this kids' website for helpful information about warts.

INDEX

Page numbers in **boldface** are illustrations.

ABOUT THE AUTHOR

Award-winning author Elaine Landau has written more than three hundred books for young readers. Many of them are on health and science topics.

Landau received a bachelor's degree in English and journalism from New York University and a master's degree in library and information science from Pratt Institute. You can visit Elaine Landau at her website: www.elainelandau.com.